The Pacific Western Group
of Companies Guide to:

OUR JOURNEY TO WORLD TO WORLD CLASS SAFETY

The Pacific Western Group
of Companies Guide to:

OUR JOURNEY
TO WORLD
CLASS SAFETY

GROUP OF COMPANIES

STEPHEN EVANS

Tellwell Talent
www.tellwell.ca
ISBN
978-0-2288-4946-9 (Paperback)
978-0-2288-4947-6 (eBook)

DEDICATION

This book is dedicated to all those working in the safety field, trying to help companies and people do things better. It is a challenging job, and often does not get much recognition.

As a safety guy, I wish sometimes I had super powers so I could swoop in to save the day and fix whatever was wrong.

Although I can't offer you any super powers, hopefully something in this book will help you to make a difference. And that is good enough for me.

ACKNOWLEDGMENTS

A special thanks goes out to Michael Colborne, Chairman and CEO of the Pacific Western Group of Companies. It was Mike who decided to hire me (great choice Mike!). It was Mike's passion and commitment that made this safety journey a reality. And it was Mike who ensured that we had the people and resources needed to reach our objective of world class safety. Thanks for all your support Mike.

And special thanks also goes to Tom Jezersek, the current President and COO of the Pacific Western Group of Companies. As Tom transitioned into the role of President a few years ago, he was handed the safety baton from Mike. And without missing a beat, Tom ran with it. He was there 100% of the time and helped the Lines and Branches carry the ball over the finish line. He then was instrumental in ensuring the transition to our next steps went without a hiccup. Thanks for your support Tom.

Thank you to my friend, Locke Marshall, for editing, proofreading, and for your suggestions. You made this a better book.

Lastly, a special thanks goes out to my wife, Linda, who put up with me being down in my basement office for hours and hours trying to accurately capture details about this journey. Thank you my love.

ASSORTED QUOTES

"We will not advance Safety at PWT by quoting rules, outlining specifications, and focusing on the technicalities.

Safety needs to connect with people and be promoted".

"Clear and concise gets the best results - not artificially formal, not using long words, not pages and pages of useless details, and not using insider acronyms".

"Stephen's approach to Safety at PWT:

- *Keep it simple*
- *Keep it real*
- *Keep it clear*
- *Keep it positive"*

"The Black Hat Approach - focuses on the errors of individuals, blaming them for forgetfulness, inattention, & stupidity.

The White Hat Approach - accepts that humans are fallible, and errors are to be expected, even in the best organizations, and recognizes that systems are required to minimize the number and severity of mistakes".

"Our internal investigations need to go deeper and look beyond the driver.

We need to find the root causes, the whys, which are almost always about the system".

"Our success in Safety will come from matching our efforts to our organization, and from focusing on what we can fix".

"Trying to fix everything, or trying to do a lot of things all at the same time often results in limited progress.

Instead we should pick a very specific safety target, then put all our energy, time, and resources towards accomplishing that target.

We'll make more progress by fixing just one thing at a time".

"Human error is:

- *Normal*
- *Inevitable*
- *Almost never intentional"*

"Seems to me that trainers would be far more successful at changing behavior if they were in the loop with safety, and knew the specific areas they should be targeting".

"Collisions, falls, trips, strains, & cuts are not random acts of fate.

- *They are predictable*
- *They can be controlled*
- *They can be prevented"*

"For me, the bottom line for driver training is about developing competencies in drivers that will reduce the possibility of them being involved in a collision, an incident, or a violation".

"Our success in attracting the right people, having them stay with us, and having them perform well hinges on our Managers knowing them, engaging them, listening to them, and responding to them".

TABLE OF CONTENTS

SECTION 1: OUR APPROACH, OUR STYLE

SECTION 2: OUR PROGRAMS, OUR INITIATIVES

SECTION 3: OUR RESULTS

SECTION 4: NEXT STEPS

SECTION 5: FINAL WORDS

INTRODUCTION

Welcome to "Our Journey to World Class Safety".

To set the stage for our story - I joined the Pacific Western Group of Companies (also called Pacific Western Transportation, or just PWT), as their VP of Safety in October of 2008. PWT operates a variety of motorcoach, school bus, and transit bus companies throughout much of Canada, and charters into the USA.

The company had ambitious plans to grow the business, but with their decentralized structure there wasn't a lot of coordination between Branches. A few of the larger Branches had a full time safety person, but for the most part safety was a part time function, sometimes added to a trainer or someone in HR. As a result there was little sharing of safety programs and initiatives throughout the group of PWT companies.

In early 2008 the President of PWT met with the Line of Business VPs to discuss how the company was going to move safety forward. He felt strongly that exemplary safety should be the hallmark of the Pacific Western brand. And he had decided that it was safety that should differentiate PWT from the competition.

Discussions eventually led to a recognition that they needed a VP of Safety to assist them with their objectives. They needed someone at a senior level who could establish a more coordinated, more visible, and more effective program.

With that as a context, after an extensive search, I was invited to join the PWT executive team, and was given a two part mandate:

- help improve safety performance across all parts of the PWT organization

- help PWT become the industry leader in bus and motorcoach safety

So we embarked on our trip together and started developing strategies as well as a game plan on how to put those strategies into action. Step by step progress was made. Year by year we steadily moved forward until we successfully accomplished both objectives in late 2018.

This book provides an overview of the trip. It highlights both the safety programs and initiatives that were put in place, as well as the approaches and styles we used to manage and improve safety performance.

Although the original objective of this book was to capture, document, and preserve details about PWT safety programs, and about their journey. We also hope it will be of some value to others in our industry. Perhaps some of the things we tried will help you strengthen and move your transportation safety programs forward as well.

It's a great story, and it is an important part of PWT's culture and history. Perhaps pieces of it will become part of your story too.

"Our Journey to World Class Safety" has been divided into Sections. Just like a story, there is a beginning (where we set the scene for the things to come); a middle (describing where we went, what we did, and the battles we fought); and a happy ending (where we celebrate the great results, and lay out our next steps).

Whether you read it from start to finish, or just jump in and out of the chapters of interest, we hope you enjoy the trip. We certainly did.

Stephen Evans

SECTION 1.

Our Approach, Our Style

CHAPTER 1.

Safety is our first Core Value

Kentucky Fried Chicken uses a secret blend of herbs and spices. The Coca Cola recipe is locked up in a vault. The Dr. Pepper recipe has been split in half and is secured in separate safes in opposite parts of the country. The recipe for Heinz Ketchup is a long held secret. And apparently we still don't know how they get the caramel into the middle of a Caramilk Bar.

However, what we can reveal in this book is how what started as a small school bus company with a fleet of 37 school buses has evolved into one of the largest bus and motorcoach companies in North America with a fleet of 5,000 buses operating out of approximately 70 facilities across Canada.

The recipe for this success has been the PWT "Core Values". There are ten: Safety, Customer Service, Resourcefulness, Integrity, Positive Attitude, Teamwork, Loyalty, Accountability, Respect, and Dedication.

This set of attributes defines the PWT organization, guiding every action and decision made by their people, informing, and supporting everything they do. It is the ultimate policy manual. No matter how small the operation, no matter how remote, the Core Values help every person in every part of the organization move things forward in the same direction, using the same value system.

All PWT staff are expected to walk the talk, and to use the Core Values in their daily tasks. The Core Values guide and inform everything at PWT.

And Safety is the first Core Value. It represents unwavering dedication to getting things right, every time. It is the one thing that is top of mind at every location in every situation.

CHAPTER 2.

Safely Home

In the early years PWT's founder, Bob Colborne, took the approach that the individual Brands should for the most part look after themselves. He expected the local managers to run the operation as if it were theirs. And so the PWT organizational structure was decentralized, and each Brand was somewhat autonomous. Bob didn't want to talk about the parent company too much as he felt the focus should be on the Brands delivering the service.

The upside of that approach was that local staff felt a sense of ownership on how things were run. They made many of the day to day decisions, and developed close ties with their communities and with their staff.

The downside was that they didn't know much about their sister Brands, or about the PWT organization as a whole. In fact in some cases they didn't even realize that other bus brands they came across on the road were actually part of the Pacific Western Group.

Eventually there was a recognition that it was time to break down some of the decentralized silos and have the Brands start talking to each other more. It was at that point that I joined PWT, and we started to develop a game plan to make safety far more visible throughout all the Brands.

At a 2009 Strategy Meeting the Executive met together to workshop how we might create a company-wide safety initiative that all Brands could participate in without bumping into any of their local programs.

As various ideas were kicked around, we landed on the notion of a new tag line – a slogan that could be added to every Brand. It would link all the companies together without disturbing existing community connections.

In what turned out to be a stroke of inspiration, we came up with the slogan: "Safely Home".

Here was an initiative that all parts of the company could get behind. Yes, work is important, but it is at home where we live most of our lives, with family and friends. Getting ourselves, our passengers, and our coworkers "Safely Home" every day is probably the most important thing a transportation company can do. And it was something the Brands had already been doing well for some time.

The next step was consulting with graphic designers, and trying out a couple different styles of logo. Eventually we landed on a logo everyone thought was a great fit, and our new "Safely Home" logo was added to every existing PWT Brand. A logo that would unify the company behind a common safety program, and would finally link the Brands and Branches together into a common PWT family.

"Safely Home" became one of the most important things we did to move safety forward at PWT. It was enthusiastically embraced by all staff, and had a big impact on many of our clients. And to ensure no other company could "borrow" the concept, we trademarked the logo both in Canada and the USA.

We occasionally even observed some of our drivers actually stopping to touch the "Safely Home" logo as they boarded their bus - making a visceral, emotional connection with the promise.

CHAPTER 3.

Safety Vision

Now that we had a "Safely Home" logo, we wanted to make sure we were all talking about it in the same way. In particular we wanted to ensure that potential clients and customers, who may not know much about PWT, knew what the "Safely Home" initiative was all about.

So again the Executive came together and workshopped some words that would describe what "Safely Home" meant to us. A Vison Statement was developed that would help those seeing the logo for the first time understand what it was all about.

Our Safety Vision

 is our deep conviction to Safety and the ultimate promise we make to each other, to our clients, and to the communities in which we operate.

The Pacific Western Group of Companies is driven by safety. It is our first Core Value, and is at the heart of all we do.

CHAPTER 4.

Safely Home Moment

Although the "Safely Home" logo showed up on our fleet of buses and motorcoaches, and the "PWT Safety Vision" poster showed up in our office reception areas, we wondered how we could extend the "Safely Home" message to other parts of our day to day work.

Enter the "Safely Home Moment". We asked all our staff, whenever they were about to start a meeting, to first have someone offer a quick safety tip that would help remind us of our "Safely Home" commitment. A safety suggestion to reinforce and keep that promise top of mind.

As an example, the "Safely Home Moment" I often use when putting on presentations, either at PWT facilities or at other venues, is a reminder about emergency exits. Most of us never think it is going to happen to us. But I always encourage participants to know where the fire exits are and how to get out of the building in the event of an emergency.

Emergency evacuation procedures are also an important part of every bus and motorcoach driver's training. And I remind them to take a moment each morning to review what they would do if a fire broke out while they were transporting a full load of passengers.

Furthermore, I challenge them to do the same thing with their families at home. Fire departments estimate that after your smoke detector goes off, you only have a handful of minutes before you could be overcome by smoke or fumes. So everyone in your family should know in an emergency how to get of every room in the home.

And I make this personal. Whenever I travel and stay at a hotel, I check to see where the fire exit is and where the stairs are. Before retiring I put out my keys, my wallet, my shoes, and my clothes on a chair - all the things I'm going to need in a hurry if the fire alarm goes off. Which in fact over the years has happened on several of my trips.

Some of the other "Safely Home Moments" used by our staff include remembering to turn on the headlight switch in daytime low visibility so the taillights go on; doing a walk around your vehicle before getting in to ensure nothing is in the way; when your vehicle starts to fishtail or slide on icy roads put it in neutral which will get the wheels turning again until you regain control, etc.

Using "Safely Home Moments" at the start of every meeting is another way of demonstrating that safety is our first Core Value, and takes priority over anything that is being discussed at the meeting.

"Safely Home Moments" are most effective when they are practical, actionable, and not just finger wagging.

CHAPTER 5.

Safety Has to Fit

In a pinch, have you ever borrowed someone else's shoes, pants, shirt, or jacket and found they didn't fit? Although better than nothing, sloshing around or being uncomfortably squeezed in someone else's clothes makes it hard to make much progress.

Similarly, companies come in all different sizes, types, and cultures. Some are about rules and regulations, others about relationships. Some are run top down, others by consensus. Some focus on sales volumes, others on quality ratings. Some are slow to change, others are always charging full speed ahead. Some like quiet traditions, others noisily push the envelope.

The point is that none of these organizational types or management styles are necessarily right or wrong. It's just that when safety programs and initiatives are being considered, they must match the organization in which they will be used.

There is no one "right" safety program. And there is no one best "best practice". Safety specialists need to keep their type of organization and their company's management style in mind when introducing new programs and initiatives. More lasting progress will be made by working within the existing company culture (even if safety staff don't think it is very good yet) than trying to force them to fit into a program that has been developed for someone else.

Sounds simple enough, but I'm amazed how many times I see safety staff who learn about a real nifty safety initiative that worked well at another organization, who then simply try to photocopy it and implement it back at their company. Unless it was developed for the same type and style of culture, it probably isn't going to get the same result.

Don't get me wrong, safety specialists should be like sponges - constantly sopping up information about the successful safety programs and initiatives of other organizations. But the trick is then to take those learnings and adapt them, adjust them, and tailor them to the type of organization where those safety specialists work.

CHAPTER 6.

Safety Does Not Own Safety

Some companies and some safety staff might disagree, but in reality, "Safety" is not owned by the Safety Department.

For example, some companies use safety staff as they would a plumber. The sales department makes unrealistic promises, and then the operations department pushes the frontline staff to deliver. And sure enough, once in a while things get plugged up and there is a mess to look after.

So they call in the safety guy or gal. And just like a plumber, safety staff have specialized training and specialized tools. They roll up their sleeves, clean up the mess, and get the sink (or worse, the toilet) working again. Once finished they are dismissed and return to their cubicle. And the sales and ops teams then go back to what they were doing before. And the cycle repeats itself year after year.

That is not the PWT approach. Our safety specialists are more like the coach of a sports team. Safety can be a resource and we can be a reminder. We can lay out the rules of the game and we can make suggestions on how to score more points. We have a playbook that can help identify the roles for each member of the team and how each player working together will accomplish the objective. We can demonstrate what could be done, when, and by whom as the team tries to move the play down the field.

But once the whistle blows, we run off the field and onto the sidelines. All we can do after that is just observe. It is the frontline operations staff who are actually on the field, playing the game, doing the work.

And they are the ones responsible for the safety of themselves and of their team. Safety is not owned by the Safety Department.

CHAPTER 7.

Move Beyond the Black Hat

As I'm sure you can tell already, I use analogies a lot in my work. This one really seemed to connect with people. I called it "Black Hat vs. White Hat".

Back in the olden days of my youth, many movie theatres showed cheap Saturday movie matinees, which were generally low budget B movies for younger viewers. Cowboy movies were particularly popular and featured heroes such as The Lone Ranger, Cisco Kid, Zorro, Sky King, Texas Rangers, and so on.

The Hollywood convention back then was that the good guys in cowboy films wore white hats, and the bad guys wore black hats. So without much help you can probably figure out this analogy.

In safety the "Black Hat" approach is about focusing on blame, of being critical of people who make mistakes, of seeing people as being not too bright, and of relying on the disciplinary process to force compliance. This is the "safety cop" type of approach.

You've probably met a few of those types. They arrive on your doorstep with a visi-vest, hard hat, steel toed boots, a pocket pen protector full of different colors of pens, a clipboard, and a thick rule book. Within 10 minutes of their arrival they are already telling you how to properly run your business.

We even had a few of those at PWT. But generally it's not our style. We lean towards a "White Hat" approach. Even with the best of intentions, sometimes people make mistakes. For us, it's not so much about who made the mistake, it's more about finding out how and why, which often leads us to look beyond the person and instead to examine systems and processes.

For example, a few years back one of our Branches was having lots of parking lot dings. Drivers were knocking off mirrors, backing into fences, scratching bumper corners, and side-swiping the bus next to them.

The Branch's first response was to get mad at the driver, start the disciplinary process, warn them it better not happen again, and schedule them into a defensive driving training course.

But when safety was invited in to figure out what was going on, we found there were no painted parking stall lines, no wheel stops in the parking stalls, and limited lighting in the yard. Once those were addressed, the number of incidents dropped drastically.

The same thing happened again at a different Branch where mechanics were shuttling buses to and from the shop for service. They kept knocking off mirrors and hitting shop door bollards. Once again, the first response by the Branch was to blame and get after the mechanics.

But the real problem was that this was an old shop with narrow doors requiring a motorcoach to be lined up perfectly before entering. The mechanics, not being experienced drivers, and not driving a coach very often, didn't know how to get the motorcoach lined up correctly. And because the driver seat on a motorcoach is forward of the steering axle, they often misjudged their turns.

The fix was painting a line on the parking lot for each bay which signified when to start the turn for that bay. Problem solved.

The Black Hat Approach focuses on blaming individuals for inattention, forgetfulness, mistakes, & stupidity - and the fix is discipline.

The White Hat Approach accepts that humans are fallible, and errors are to be expected, even in the best organizations - and recognizes that systems and processes are required to minimize the number and severity of mistakes

And let's talk about discipline a little bit. Simply put it has no place in safety.

The discipline process should be looked after by the worker's supervisor. If an employee keeps showing up late, is caught stealing, or is bullying other employees, the supervisor can follow up using the standard four step disciplinary process (verbal warning, written warning, suspension, termination).

But people don't willingly have collisions or incidents. These are not the same as poor behavior. You can't stop people making mistakes by punishing them. And as soon as you ask safety staff to get involved in disciplining drivers, you'll lose all credibility - nobody will report anything for fear of it blowing back on them.

Safety should not do discipline.

To paraphrase a quote I read somewhere many years ago, "An accident or incident should be seen as an opportunity to learn, not as a reason to punish".

CHAPTER 8.

Top of the Cliff

Another of our signature analogies we call – "Spend Time On Top Of The Cliff".

If you can imagine a twisty road that runs along the top of a steep cliff, you can occasionally see drivers that aren't paying attention, maybe going too fast, or are arguing with the person in the passenger seat. Possibly they are reaching to change the radio station, or maybe texting on their phone. For a variety of reasons they aren't paying attention. They miss a tight turn, slide off the road, go over the edge, and come crashing down at the bottom of the cliff.

A lot of traditional safety programs focus on that bottom of the cliff. They look after Emergency Response, Recovery, and an Investigation.

Safety staff love this stuff. We actually get to do something. We get noticed. We get to drive vehicles with flashing lights, and wear official looking uniforms.

In some companies the safety department is normally almost invisible. They are only called on when something bad happens.

Of course there is no argument that we need to do a good job at the bottom of the cliff. PWT developed a comprehensive post collision swim lane chart that outlined all of the various roles, and shows who does what when as the response unfolds. This included the Driver, Dispatcher, Operations Manager, Insurance Adjuster, Safety Staff, Corporate Office, and Insurance Claims Dept. who all work together in a coordinated effort.

To assist in that response, recovery, and investigation process, PWT developed a number of tools such as a standardized collision report template and an on-line tablet based reporting app.

So yes, PWT takes very seriously their responsibility for looking after things at the bottom of the cliff. But surely the more important priority for safety staff should be up on top of the cliff - building fences and helping prevent drivers from falling off the cliff in the first place. Some of those fences might be training, standard operating procedures, awareness programs, and the like.

The aviation industry learned this lesson some time ago. In the early years of manned flight they used to prang up planes pretty regularly. And people got hurt. In October of 1935 Boeing was putting on a big show for the US Army Air Corp showing off a brand new plane, the B-17 Flying Fortress. But shortly after take-off it nose-dived into the ground and caught on fire, killing several on board.

The investigation found that the plane was in perfect condition. But the flight crew had forgotten to release the gust control lock that kept things from flapping around in the wind while parked on the ground.

Out of that investigation came the recognition that there were just too many things to do for a person to remember on their own. So the "checklist" was developed as a tool to help guide a pilot, step by step, through the process of getting a plane ready for flight.

From then on checklists became mandatory and are now used in every phase of flight. Also the use of a checklist has expanded beyond aviation and is now being by hospitals, architects, educators, software developers, etc.

Whether we are a pilot in a cockpit that is getting ready to take off, a surgeon in an operating room about to remove a patient's gall bladder, or a bus driver sitting behind the wheel about to enter the freeway during rush hour, we are all the same, we are all fallible humans. We have short memories, we get distracted easily, and we are prone to occasionally slipping up.

At PWT we moved our safety team to the top of the cliff. We directed them to help develop processes and systems that would prevent or minimize mistakes.

Although the singer John Denver was not a safety guy, he often recited this poem during his shows which highlights a top of the cliff approach:

THE AMBULANCE DOWN IN THE VALLEY

T'was a dangerous cliff as they freely confessed
though to walk near its edge was so pleasant.
But over its edge had slipped a Duke,
and it fooled many a peasant.
The people said something would have to be done
but their projects did not at all tally.
Some said, "put a fence around the edge of the cliff,"
others, "an ambulance down in the valley."
The lament of the crowd was profound and loud
as their hearts overflowed with pity.
But the ambulance carried the cry of the day

as it spread to the neighboring cities.
So a collection was made to accumulate aid
and dwellers in highway and alley,
gave dollars and cents not to furnish a fence,
but an ambulance down in the valley.
For the cliff is alright if you're careful they said,
and if folks ever slip and are falling;
it's not the slipping and falling that hurts them
so much as the shock down below when they're stopping.
And so for years as these mishaps occurred
quick forth would the rescuers sally,
to pick up the victims who fell from the cliff
with the ambulance down in the valley.
Said one in his plea, it's a marvel to me
that you'd give so much greater attention
to repairing results than to curing the cause, why
you'd much better aim at prevention.
For the mischief of course should be stopped at its source;
come friends and neighbors let us rally.
It makes far better sense to rely on a fence
than an ambulance down in the valley.
He's wrong in his head the majority said.
He would end all our earnest endeavors.
He's the kind of a man that would shrink his responsible work,
but we will support it forever.
Aren't we picking up all just as fast as they fall,
and giving them care liberally.
Why a superfluous fence is of no consequence,
if the ambulance works in the valley.

Now this story seems queer as I've given it here,
but things oft occur which are stranger.
More humane we assert to repair all the hurt,
than the plan of removing the danger.
The best possible course would be to safeguard the source,
and to attend to things rationally.
Yes, build up the fence and let us dispense
with this ambulance down in the valley.

CHAPTER 9.

Crystal Clear

I love movies, and one of the classics for me is "A Few Good Men" starring Tom Cruise, Jack Nicholson, and Demi Moore. You might remember the court room scene where Jack Nicholson is playing the part of Base Commander Colonel Nathan Jessup, who is on the stand defending charges of covering up a Code Red murder on the base.

Tom Cruise is a Junior Grade Lieutenant assigned to cross-exam Colonel Jessup. As the Lieutenant hammers away at the Colonel about whether Marines always follow orders, the scene comes to a climax with a seething Colonel, declaring through clenched teeth that, "We Follow Orders, Or People Die! ARE WE CLEAR"?

Cruise answers, "Yes, sir". Again the Colonel, making his point, emphatically asks, "ARE WE CLEAR"? And Cruise answers - "CRYSTAL"!

That is what we want our safety programs and safety initiatives to be - Crystal Clear. We have to make sure all of our staff completely understand what it is we are trying to encourage them to do. Our materials need to be practical, clear, and real.

We find sometimes that safety folks can ramble on a bit. They tend to use long words and acronyms. And if something can be said in one sentence, they'll find ways to have it take up a whole page.

There are lots of different personalities in every company. Some folks are very linear and organized. They like things with a beginning, a middle, and an end. Other folks are more organic. They tend to be all over the map, and kind of just go with the flow.

We realized that to get the results we were looking for, we would need to be clear and concise so that we reached every type of personality.

We encouraged our safety staff to use the "passerby test". This means that if I'm putting together a policy, program, or document, once finished I should be able to give it to any stranger that happens to be walking down the street, and they should easily be able to understand what it is about, and what it is asking the reader to do.

My approach to Safety at PWT is to:

- Keep it simple
- Keep it practical
- Keep it clear
- Keep it positive

To get the best possible results, all safety processes, procedures, policies, and materials produced should be – "CRYSTAL CLEAR"!

CHAPTER 10.

Red Flags

The term "Red Flags" is often used to describe early warnings signs. These are issues, problems, or concerns, that although small now, could easily turn into something more major if ignored.

I think one of the coolest military aircraft is the AWACS. This acronym stands for Airborne Warning And Control System. These planes are equipped with a large round radar device called a radome, and are up patrolling the edges of our continent 24/7.

Their sophisticated radar systems continually scan the skies for red flags - possible incursions into the North American airspace by the bad guys. In the event that something is discovered heading our way, the AWACS give us adequate time to respond and either eliminate, or at least minimize the threat.

Bus and motorcoach companies can likewise use the information and data they collect to discover their own red flags. It might be an increasing percentage of staff turnover, the poor results from a customer satisfaction survey, or several unreported violations on a driver's license abstract.

The FMCSA (Federal Motor Carrier Safety Administration) in the USA has lots of data about commercial vehicle drivers, and about accidents involving commercial vehicles. In a report published a few years ago they showed that statistically, a commercial vehicle driver who had a prior accident, was 87% more likely than the average commercial vehicle driver to have another accident. That is quite a red flag.

What would you do if that was one of your drivers, if you discovered that a driver in your workforce had recently had an accident? According to the FMCSA stats, that driver would now apparently be more at risk of having another collision in the future.

Would you just try to get rid of that person? If so, that might not help very much, as the replacement is likely to be just another person with a red flag in their background as well.

If your safety program depends on finding perfect professional drivers, you are in for a big disappointment. That's not reality, especially today where we often seem to have a shortage of commercial vehicle drivers.

Instead, you might consider using red flags to help proactively focus on developing and delivering better training, better processes, and better systems.

This concept was covered really well in a popular business book. The author's research found over and over again, that great companies had put in place a system to watch out for, listen to, and follow up on red flags.

Red flags should be an immediate call for action. The quicker you can identify an issue that is taking you away from your safety objectives; and the quicker you can develop and implement a response; the more likely you will reach your safety performance targets. And seldom will your programs get ambushed or hijacked.

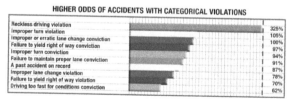

HIGHER ODDS OF ACCIDENTS WITH CATEGORICAL VIOLATIONS

Reckless driving violation	325%
Improper turn violation	105%
Improper or erratic lane change conviction	100%
Failure to yield right of way conviction	97%
Improper turn conviction	94%
Failure to maintain proper lane conviction	91%
A past accident on record	87%
Improper lane change violation	78%
Failure to yield right of way violation	70%
Driving too fast for conditions conviction	62%

CHAPTER 11.

Steak vs. Sizzle

If you were planning to open a restaurant specializing in steak, you could advertise your new venture in one of two ways.

You could post an ad displaying the various cuts of meat; which grades and marbling you offer; the breeds of cattle you purchase; an overview of how the supplier responsibly raises their cattle; and details of how the meat is dry aged.

Or…

You could simply display a photo of attractive young couples sitting around a table, with a delicious steaming feast in front of them, laughing among themselves and giving a toast.

Which ad do you think will get the best response? I'm guessing most of us would pick the photo of the couples enjoying themselves, sitting in front of a delicious meal.

Why? Because the first ad is just relaying facts and figures, while the second ad makes an emotional connection. As we see the tendrils of steam coming off the steak, and see the butter melting over the mashed potatoes, our mouth begins to water, and we can almost taste the meal. We relate to visiting with friends and having a great evening together. We want to go to place that offers that experience.

I call that the "Sizzle".

If it comes down to a description of the "Steak" vs. an image of the "Sizzle" - the sizzle wins hands down every time.

Safety is no different. But we often find that safety staff get so wrapped up in the technical facts and figures that they forget that safety needs to be promoted.

We can't just simply develop a safety program, initiative, or process and then expect the technical details will be enough for people to get it and do it.

Just as with our restaurant example, safety needs to find ways to promote the "Sizzle" - to make those emotional connections that motivate and influence behavior.

CHAPTER 12.

Beware of Icebergs

At 11:40 pm on April 14, 1912 the technological marvel of the industrial age, the "unsinkable" Titanic, hit an iceberg and a few hours later sank to the bottom of the Atlantic Ocean.

She had entered known iceberg waters at full speed on a moonless night and did not respond to telegraph warnings from five other ships about icebergs in her path.

The Titanic was equipped with the best of what modern engineering at the time had to offer. But detailed investigations identified the one hazard that had not been eliminated, poor judgment.

But this chapter is not about how poor judgment has been at the root of some of the world's biggest disasters. Instead we want to talk about icebergs.

The thing about an iceberg is that you only see a small part of it. Up to 90% of an iceberg sits below the waves. What we can see above the water may not look very imposing, but if we are not careful there is a large amount of grief waiting for us just below the surface.

The same holds true for our "minor" collisions. When a big loss occurs it is all hands on deck, with investigations, photos, interviews, witness statements, and the like. But it is easy to dismiss small parking lot collisions. We sometimes just don't bother with a full response because, "It's just a minor ding".

Maybe we think knocking off mirrors, backing into fences, and clipping poles is an inevitable cost of doing business. Maybe we don't even capture them in our accident register - wrong approach! If left unchecked these can turn into your very own iceberg.

You might think that the cost of replacing a mirror is just a couple of dollars. But there are a lot of other unseen expenses involved in replacing that mirror: downtime while the unit is not able to generate revenue; the time/effort to discover the problem and write it up/submit it to the shop; and the costs associated with either stocking or purchasing that mirror. Also someone has to drive the unit in to and out of the shop; that service bay is no longer available to be used for other work; plus there is a lot of administrative paperwork around generating and filing a work order. Often the repair is just coded as a maintenance cost instead of an accident anyway - Yikes!

Insurance company studies show that for every $1 spent on direct costs such as parts and labour, there are at least $3 - $5 spent on indirect, behind the scenes (under the water) costs.

So - watch out for icebergs. If you don't respond to parking lot dings as you would with any other accident, you are going to find that these "minor" dings are costing you "major" bucks.

CHAPTER 13.

Sniper vs. Shotgun

You might have come across the humorous poster showing a safety officer holding a hammer, with the caption, "To a safety officer with a hammer, everything looks like a nail".

It has a ring of truth about it because it is really easy for safety staff to feel they are responsible to watch out for and fix every single problem in an organization. Sort of like my childhood cartoon hero Mighty Mouse, who proclaimed, "Here I come to save the day"!

The reality is that those types of safety programs, and those types of safety staff mostly just spin their wheels, and soon burn out from the burden of trying to be everywhere and trying to fix everything. They may make a bit of noise trying, but nothing really changes.

Early on in our journey we used the analogy of "Sniper vs. Shotgun". The notion being that it was far more effective to use a sophisticated measurement instrument, like a rifle scope, to clearly identify a specific target, and then put all your focus on dealing with that one problem, before moving on to the next.

The shotgun approach is where you spread your efforts over many issues. You point your initiatives in a general direction, and then hope that maybe, just maybe, a few of the fixes actually connect.

This is one of the most difficult things for a safety specialist to do. No matter how experienced, how well trained, or how well equipped, a safety specialist cannot solve all problems all at the same time. You are going to have to let some things slide. The best value you can provide is to focus on one thing at a time.

Another similar analogy we call "Focused Finding and Fixing".

In this one we have you imagine that you are walking barefoot on Kitsilano Beach in Vancouver and step on a piece of driftwood. Ouch, you get a wood splinter in your big toe, which now makes it very difficult to complete your walk because it hurts like heck!

So what are things you would need to look after that toe and get you back on your walk?

- a magnifying glass to find the splinter
- antiseptic to clean the area
- a pair of tweezers so you can pull the splinter out
- ointment to promote healing
- a Band-Aid to protect the area from future harm.

Observation #1. If you don't have and use the right tools for the job, you may not be able to respond to the problem very well. For example, a pair of Channellock pliers might look a little like an overgrown pair of tweezers, but they won't get the splinter out, unless you take a large chunk of toe with it!

Observation #2. Even with the right tools, they must be used in the right way, and in the right order, and for the right target. For example applying the Band Aid first, before pulling out the splinter, is not going to relieve your pain.

What PWT learned from these two analogies was to approach collisions and incidents in a far more focused process. Using our safety performance metrics we identify a specific area of concern. Then we apply our energy and resources to resolve that one specific target. We don't try to fix everything all at once.

Here is one of my favorite quotes by Thomas S. Monson, *"When we deal in generalities, we shall never succeed. When we deal in specifics, we shall rarely have a failure".*

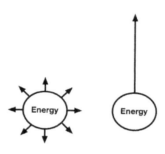

SECTION 2.

Our Programs, Our Initiatives

CHAPTER 14.

KPI (Key Performance Indicators)

Here is another of my favorite quotes, also by Thomas S. Monson, *"When performance is measured, performance improves. When performance is measured and reported, the rate of improvement accelerates".*

Right from the start of "Our Journey To World Class Safety" we knew we needed to find a way to measure and report safety performance both at the Branch level, then rolled up into the Line of Business level, and finally into a Corporate total.

Our decentralized group of companies, with several dozen Branches, in a number of provinces, and organized into four Lines of Business, were all operating somewhat independently from each other. They tended to measure the things that made sense for their operation, often in slightly different ways from other Branches, even within their own Line of Business.

We started out by looking at all the different types of data being captured across the entire organization. We found that even though it was measured a little differently, everyone was capturing some information about Collisions, WCB claims, Breakdowns, Lates, and

Staff Turnover. So that's what we started with. Each month each Branch would send in their numbers for those categories, and we assembled these into a monthly summary report.

We recognized we needed a short, punchy, and easy to remember term for this new monthly safety reporting process, a term that everyone would understand and connect with our safety performance.

Although the term Key Performance Indicators can be used for all types of important business data, we decided that at PWT we would use the term primarily for safety, and so our "KPI" program was born.

Now at last we could begin to see each month how we were doing in safety throughout all parts of the company - both with the individual Branches, by the Lines of Business, and with the Company as a whole.

However, this somewhat shaky start only allowed for month over month comparisons for individual Branches, and didn't allow much comparison between Branches of different sizes and types. So it didn't take long until we were separating Collisions into Preventable Collisions vs. Non-Preventable Collisions, which then allowed us to calculate the Preventable Collisions per Million Mile Rate (the most common safety performance measure for road transport). Now we were able to compare apples to apples, Branch against Branch, Line against Line, and Company against the industry.

It took several years of fine tuning the definitions, and we added several new categories along the way, including the TIF (total injury frequency) rate. But the turning point came when the Finance/ Accounting Dept. agreed to take over the collection, compiling, and reporting of our monthly KPI.

The Finance Team specializes in numbers. And it has the expertise, the systems, and the software horsepower to both collect, crunch, and report out lots of numbers reliably, accurately, consistently, and on time every month.

After the Finance team took over the management of KPI reporting, we started getting monthly reports showing performance for several prior months, the current month, the year to date, and the prior year to date. And from there was no looking back. The Finance Dept. breathed life into our KPI, which now took on a new and more significant role in how PWT was managed.

Here is the list of KPI categories we eventually decided to capture, along with their definitions. The bottom five are not really KPI as much as they are raw numbers needed to calculate the Turnover rate, TIF rate, and Preventable Collision rate.

PWT KPI Definitions

Preventable Collisions: Any contact between a PWT revenue producing vehicle and anything else, where our driver could have done something to prevent it from happening.

Non-Preventable Collisions: Any contact between a PWT revenue producing vehicle and anything else, where our driver could not have done something to prevent it from happening.

Driver Violations: Tickets issued to our driver for infractions of Federal, Provincial, State, or Municipal regulations as a result of their operating a PWT revenue producing vehicle.

Injury Incidents: Any injury occurring at work resulting in first aid treatment by another employee or first aider, or that warrants medical evaluation following an initial self-administered treatment.

Workers Compensation Claims: Any harm to an employee that results in a claim being opened by a Workers Compensation Board, excluding "Notice Only Claims".

Workers Compensation Lost Days: Any regularly scheduled workdays missed by an employee as a result of a Workers Compensation Claim.

Small Group Safety Meetings: A facility safety meeting where:

- Safety is the main focus
- There are no less than 3 and no more than 12 attendees consisting of shop staff and/or drivers
- The meeting is at least 15 minutes in length
- A frontline Supervisor takes the lead
- Minutes and attendance are documented

Lates: Any delay to service at the beginning of a trip that exceeds the first scheduled departure time by at least 5 minutes (does not include subsequent delays during the trip).

Breakdowns: A mechanical failure of a PWT revenue producing vehicle while enroute.

Complaints: Any communication from our passengers or the public in any form expressing discontent with our service and/or organization.

Turnover Rate: "Resignations/Terminations" divided by "Total # of Staff" shown as a percentage to one decimal point.

TIF Rate: "Injury Incidents" multiplied by 200,000, divided by "Total Hours Worked" to two decimal points.

Preventable Collisions per Million Miles Rate: "Preventable Collisions" divided by "Usage (Miles)" multiplied by 1,000,000 to one decimal.

Total # of Staff: The total # of employees on payroll at of the month.

Resignations/Terminations: Includes all categories of employees and all reasons except does not include layoffs, transfers to a different division, temporary workers, trainees, or retirees.

Total Hours Worked: The total hours worked by all employees during the month.

Usage (Kilometers): The total number of kilometers travelled by PWT revenue producing vehicles during the month.

Usage (Miles): The "Usage (Kilometers)" converted to miles using a conversion factor of 0.621371

CHAPTER 15.

CoS (Cost of Safety)

Once our KPI process was firmly established, we realized we only had part of the equation. The next obvious question was, "Ok, we now know how many incidents we are having every month, but what does that mean? How are we supposed to respond? What is the real impact of these KPI numbers"?

Once again, the Finance Dept. saved the day. They were able to dig out the various accounting codes used for every purchase and every cost, for every KPI category. And soon we were getting a monthly "Cost of Safety" report as a companion to the KPI Report.

It was organized into three groups of costs. Fleet Safety Costs (on road incidents), Workplace Safety Costs (workplace incidents), and Administration Costs.

Here are the categories:

Fleet Safety
- Insurance Premiums
- Insurance Deductible
- Accident Damage Repairs

- Accident Damage Repair Recoveries
- Accident Related Passenger Claims

Workplace Safety
- WCB Premiums
- WCB Rebates

Administration of Safety
- Safety Staff Wages
- Safety Supplies
- Safety Promotion
- Safety Office Supplies

Some of our safety staff argued that depicting safety as a "cost" was not the right approach because that might overshadow the human part of dealing with losses.

I hope that as you read this book you recognize PWT is absolutely all about looking after people.

It is also a reality that for our Executive and senior management team, a large part of their work is about financial numbers. So adding this Cost of Safety report provided the numbers connection that helped round out and make sense of the monthly KPI report.

CHAPTER 16.

The Balanced Scorecard

I would venture to observe that in every successful well-run company, there is a bottom-line undercurrent which flows through each and every aspect of the organization. From the Boardroom to the Bathroom, every person, in every department, in every location understands that they each have a part to play in winning/keeping customers, and ensuring it is being done profitably.

Sure, you can argue that reducing KPI incidents is a good thing and is inherently the right thing to do. But with the addition of the monthly Cost of Safety Report, the bottom-line impact of doing things well is immediately apparent.

No longer do you have to wait until the year end financials to see if something on the safety side is out of whack. The KPI Report and the companion Cost of Safety Report enables management to constantly watch over the operation, almost in real-time, and respond quickly if things start to go off track.

The Finance Dept. took this to the next level when they created "The Balanced Scorecard". They added these two safety reports to their monthly financials.

Now every month the Branches gets their Financial results in a three-part package: First the financial report, second the KPI Report, and third the Cost of Safety Report. And the same holds true for the Lines of Business results, and the overall Corporate results.

This has become what our CFO calls, "Our one source of truth". It clearly establishes and demonstrates the balance between the People part and the Financial part of PWT.

Running a large fleet of buses and motorcoaches on roads all over Canada (and a little into the USA) is a risky business. And we are never going to eliminate all collisions and all incidents. But the Balance Scorecard helps us to find the sweet spot, where we spend the right amount of money, on the right types of programs, to look after our people, and that allows the company to prosper.

It really is a balancing act. And the Balanced Scorecard helps us to do it well.

Monthly Facility Balanced Scorecard:
- Financial Results
- Safety KPI Results
- Cost of Safety Results

Our One Source of Truth !

CHAPTER 17.

Yearly & Monthly KPI & CoS Budgets

Of course, what good are performance numbers unless you have something to strive for - an objective, a target.

Each November the Branches develop a budget proposal for the next year. Not only do they develop predicted sales revenue and cost projections, they also build a budget for their anticipated KPI and Cost of Safety numbers.

Based on projected miles, the number of staff, the types of service being offered, their KPI/CoS history over the previous several years, and the safety initiatives they plan to introduce, the Branches decide on what KPI safety performance numbers they want to accomplish the coming year, together with the associated projected costs.

Additionally, to support their proposed KPI budget, they submit a "KPI Action Plan" which outlines the specific steps they will take in the coming year, identifies who will do what, lays out how it will be accomplished, provides a timeline with waypoints, and stipulates specifically how much of an improvement will result.

Once approved, these budget numbers are added into the KPI and CoS Reports for the next year. Then in the monthly reports, not only can they track month over prior month, and YTD over prior YTD performance, they can additionally compare KPI performance against their monthly and YTD budget projections.

To promote KPI accountability up and down the organization, each month, the four Line of Business VPs participate in a conference call with the President to discuss any KPI budget shortfalls, and explain what it is being done about it.

The most powerful part of our entire KPI initiative, is that the numbers are developed by the Branch - not the Corporate office, and not the Safety Dept. The Branch sets the targets, develops the action plan, monitors the results, and proactively jumps in to respond when things start to go off track.

It is a wonderful thing to observe.

CHAPTER 18.

IVMS

IVMS - four little letters that are changing motor transport.

It has been said that truck drivers and bus drivers are the last unsupervised workforce in North America. Our drivers arrive at the yard at the beginning of their shift, receive their assignment, complete their pre-trip, and then head out onto the streets. And that's it. We don't see them again until they return at the end of their shift, hopefully without harm, incident, or damage.

An often cited study by Kare Rumar, analyzing British and American crash reports, found that 57% of crashes were due solely to driver factors; 27% to combined driver and roadway factors; 6% to combined driver and vehicle factors; 3% to combined driver, roadway, and vehicle factors; 1% to combined roadway and vehicle factors; 2% solely to vehicle factors; and 3% solely to roadway factors. Therefore, according to this study, 93% of all crashes in some way involve the driver doing, or not doing, something that eventually led to a crash.

This means as our bus and motorcoach drivers head out of the yard each day, we are hoping that they defy the odds, and that our screening, our training, our procedures, our culture, etc. will help our drivers make good choices.

Enter telematics – "In Vehicle Monitoring System (IVMS)", or depending on your approach "In Vehicle Management System", or "In Vehicle Mentoring System".

The vehicle is equipped with a device that that has GPS to determine vehicle location, and it captures information on speed, cornering, braking, accelerating, engine rpm, and the driver seatbelt.

With these inputs, the unit is able to capture and send notifications in real time when:

- the driver seat belt is not being used
- the vehicle is taken out of route
- there is harsh cornering, harsh braking, or harsh acceleration
- the local speed limit is being broken
- there is extended idling, or overrevving

Most IVMS units provide a driver feedback panel which gives the driver an early heads up when they drift outside normal parameters. If the driver reacts quickly and gets back into the normal zone it is not recorded.

But if the driver does not respond, the event is captured, recorded, and sent to the dispatch office for further review and analysis.

This technology for the first time allows visibility into how a vehicle is being driven.

You might think that drivers would be concerned about "big brother" watching over their every move, but in fact, most drivers embrace the technology as it gives them an opportunity to monitor and self-manage their driving decisions and improve their style of driving.

For those who are less observant, the events captured become a driver report card that can be used to pinpoint those who are struggling. This in turn can be used for focused follow up with specific drivers.

This is a win, win, win.

- It is a win for drivers who embrace this tool which helps them fine tune their driving performance

- It is a win that at-risk drivers are identified and addressed before they turn into crashes

- It is a win for post incident training that no longer has to cover the full range of a A-to-Z defensive driving curriculum, but now can focus on the specific areas needing attention

That's a lot of wins for four little letters!

iVMS

In Vehicle Management System

CHAPTER 19.

NSC

When I first joined PWT I faced a fairly daunting challenge. How was I going to get to know, and get up to speed about all the Branches and Brands within the Pacific Western Group of Companies? How was I going to assess where things were at with safety throughout the Company?

I needed a good reason to visit each facility and peek into the various nooks and crannies. And it turned out that apparently no one had previously done an overview assessment of all the Branches. Hiccups had been dealt with primarily as a one offs at the local Branch level.

Bus and motorcoach carriers in Canada are regulated by Provincial Commercial Vehicle Fleet Safety Standards. Which are based on a set of guidelines called the National Safety Code (NSC). These guidelines provide a template on how to manage the fleet, the drivers, the shop, the safety program, and the supporting documents.

However, many/most bus and motorcoach fleets seldom operate on major highways, and so tend to be off the radar, until of course, things hit the fan. So I figured this was a good place to start in my quest to become familiar with the PWT organization.

Using an Alberta Transportation Commercial Vehicle Compliance Audit tool as the foundation, I developed our own "PWT Fleet Safety Internal Review". It contained questions about what was in the Branch safety program; how drivers were screened, hired, trained, and supervised; how vehicles were inspected, repaired, and maintained; and it also examined all the related documentation.

That first year I visited every PWT Branch and facility across Canada, and using our newly minted PWT Fleet Safety Internal Review, I was able to get a really good overview on how well we were doing with fleet safety issues across the entire organization.

Normally it takes a major accident, or an excessive number of Carrier Profile points before a carrier will get audited by Department of Transportation authorities. And of course, by then it is often too late, as the results are usually fines and/or being put on probation.

But through our PWT Fleet Safety Internal Reviews, we were able to understand how we were doing with fleet issues, and which areas needed to be strengthened. These reviews gave us a visibility and transparency into the fleet like we never had before.

We went from just keeping our fingers crossed and hoping we were OK, to absolutely knowing where we were good, and where we needed some work.

And it helped me become more familiar with the organization. I got to know the staff at each Branch, and was able to begin building the credibility we would need as we moved safety at PWT forward.

These Fleet Safety Internal Reviews were to become an annual tradition. And once again we looked for a short, simple, but punchy term we could use to describe the whole range of fleet safety compliance issues. It didn't take us long to borrow and adopt the term "NSC".

Over the years the process we use for our annual NSC reviews has evolved. But it remains one of the foundations of our safety program. Besides the obvious benefit to the local Branches, our NSC review process provides a comfort level to the Board and the Executive that all parts of the company are operating professionally, are using industry best practices, and are in compliance.

FLEET SAFETY (NSC):

1. Written Safety Plan
2. Driver Records
3. Written Vehicle Maintenance Program
4. Vehicle Records
5. Hours Of Service
6. Due Diligence

CHAPTER 20.

COR

Although most of our staff, and most of our risks are on the road, covered by "Fleet Safety" (NSC) standards and programs, there are of course the more traditional "Workplace Safety" issues that need to be looked after at our shops, our yards, and occasionally even in our offices.

So, at the same time we developed our annual NSC Internal Review program, we also started looking for a similar process we could use on the workplace side.

We found that a couple of our Branches had signed up for the Alberta Worker's Compensation Board program called "Partners in Injury Reduction". This program provides participants with a template of best practices and standards, to assist companies as they proactively strengthen their workplaces. The objective is to minimize worker injuries and of course the related WCB claims.

Participation in the program requires the company to go through an annual internal audit for the first two years, followed by successfully passing an external audit performed by a certified safety association auditor every third year. Companies are then awarded a "Certificate of Recognition (COR)", and would also receive a WCB premium rebate.

At the time only Alberta was offering this program. But it was exactly what we were looking for on the workplace safety side. And so, just as with the NSC, we borrowed the template and the audit tool, and developed our own "PWT Workplace Safety Internal Review", and then rolled it out across the entire group of companies.

And you guessed it...we soon were calling it "COR".

For many years we performed these COR reviews whether the Branch was involved in the WCB program or not. But over the years more and more provinces have started their own programs, and now every one of our Branches is participating. So we just use the official COR annual audit reports to monitor workplace safety across the organization.

WORKPLACE SAFETY (COR):
1. Management Leadership & Organizational Commitment
2. Hazard Identification & Assessment
3. Hazard Control
4. Ongoing Work Site Inspections
5. Worker Qualifications, Orientation, & Training
6. Emergency Response
7. Accident & Incident Investigation
8. Program Administration

CHAPTER 21.

Carrier Profiles

Similar to a driver's license abstract, the Carrier Profile is a complete review of every officially reported violation, inspection, and collision that occurs with your bus and motorcoach fleet. Each commercial vehicle license plate registration contains a unique company NSC number, which is how the Carrier Profile information is collected whenever police or transportation officers write up an incident.

Each event is assigned points depending on the type and severity of the event. The Carrier Profile then provides an overview of the total score for your fleet; compares your score against the industry average; and shows the threshold level that if exceeded will result in Dept. of Transportation intervention.

Obviously, the Company will know about the more significant accidents where a damaged bus has to be towed. But sometimes it is human nature that a driver might "forget" to report that they got a ticket for speeding, or running a red light, etc.

We encouraged all of our Branches to obtain their Carrier Profile regularly (at least annually), to ensure there weren't any surprises, and to ensure they didn't unknowingly trigger intervention action.

We also found, unfortunately, that sometimes when police respond to a bus vs. car accident, they tend to give the benefit of the doubt to the car, and without justification assign blame to the bus (perhaps with a misguided notion that big company = big insurance pockets).

On the carrier profile, "At Fault" accidents are penalized a larger number of points against the Company. So we emphasized to our Branches that they check every collision to ensure that it had been captured correctly. Fortunately, if caught in time, incorrectly assigned points can be appealed with a detailed submission, and most times reversed.

In addition to having our Branches pull the Carrier Profile, the PWT Safety Council also felt it would be useful take a look at Carrier Profile scores at each Council Meeting. At first, we just pulled and reviewed the numbers for our own Branches to ensure nothing was slipping through the cracks. Later we also started to pull and review the Carrier Profile scores of all the other bus and motorcoach companies we could in each Province. This allowed us to see how our safety scores were stacking up against our competitors. It also had the added bonus of providing information about fleet size, miles operated, etc., for the rest of our industry.

CHAPTER 22.

Site Visits

One of the legacies left by Bob Colborne, the founder of Pacific Western, was the Core Values. What's not to like about a company that is based on Safety, Customer Service, Resourcefulness, Integrity, Positive Attitude, Teamwork, Loyalty, Accountability, Respect, and Dedication?

Most of us felt more like we were members of the Colborne family, not just employees. That feeling of a connection with the family was felt right across the entire group of companies, even though our people were spread far and wide.

I think this is one of the reasons that the Branches got really excited when they had a visitor from the Corporate office. It helped them maintain that feeling of connectiveness. And they were pleased with the opportunity to strut their stuff, knowing that observations about their part of the PWT world would be passed onto the family.

Once the PWT Safety Council Meeting process had finally taken shape, we started to rotate our Council Meetings and hold them at locations where we had Branches throughout different parts of the company. Sometimes we visited the big Brands in the big cities, and other times we visited the smaller Brands in more remote communities.

In every case, as part of our agenda, we would break out of our meeting to visit the local Branch. We asked them to give us a tour of the facility, to show us how they had put in place the Hazardous Waste/ Recyclables Checklist, and we asked them to provide an overview of their KPI performance, highlighting how they were doing with their yearly KPI budget and corresponding KPI action plan.

This is big stuff. It puts personality, pride, and passion into programs. These visits are engaging. They build connections, and make it real.

CHAPTER 23.

Hazardous Wastes & Recyclables

Once upon a time, one of our facilities that used waste oil to heat their bus shop, found they were collecting more waste oil from bus oil changes than they were burning in the furnace. Having run out of storage space in their regular waste oil storage tank, they started using empty 45 gallon drums as temporary storage, with a plan to transfer these once they had room in the main storage tank again.

First, the drums were stacked along an unused wall in the shop. But eventually they ran out of space, and started collecting these drums of waste oil outside, at the back of the shop. As it turns out, occasionally some of the bungs (threaded plugs) on top of the drums were not installed.

Winter arrived, snows came, and the shop got very busy. Eventually once again spring approached, and the snows began to melt, but the shop had not yet got around to transferring the waste oil in those drums, and without bungs, the melting snow seeped into some of them, causing a few to overflow oily water over the side of the drum and down onto the ground.

Enter Murphy's Law. A recently hired, inexperienced Alberta Environmental Officer, apparently looking to make a name for himself, caught wind of this situation and came a calling. His interpretation was that the oil staining on the ground around the base of a few of the drums constituted a significant major spill. He was going to ensure this irresponsible shop was made an example of, to send a message to all other companies in the area - a big feather in his new enforcement hat.

It didn't matter that this region of Northern Alberta has naturally occurring oil laden dirt, gravel, and sand lying just below the surface. This officer pursued a wide variety of environmental non-compliance violation charges, including, believe it or not, criminal charges against the Vice President and the GM.

We of course hired lawyers, and fought for a more common sense response to this relatively minor staining incident that was a result of an innocent oversight by a busy shop.

We ended up getting most of the charges dropped, and paid a fine we believed was fair. But the legal bills were hundreds of thousands of dollars. All because our shop staff, probably in a hurry, forgot to install .91 cent bungs into those storage drums.

For PWT, the moral of the story was that never again were we going to allow ourselves to suffer the consequences of poor handling of hazardous recyclables.

We put together a Hazardous Wastes/Recyclables Inspection Checklist, and rolled it out to all our shops:

1. Containers of hazardous waste or recyclables
    -   must be clearly marked & labeled
    -   must be in good condition & not leaking

- should be kept closed except when adding/removing waste
- should be located to avoid damage/ruptures
- should be protected from the weather
- should be located away from sewer, storm, drainage, streams, ponds, etc.
- must have secondary containment
- must include regular inspections of the area around containers

2. Develop procedures for handling and storing hazardous waste and recyclables, including a robust spill response

3. All shop employees are to be trained on spill response

4. All stains and spills are to be cleaned up immediately

5. Each facility should have adequate spill response supplies

6. Hazardous Waste and Recyclables should be added to the facility Emergency Response Plan

And as was mentioned in the prior chapter, this became one of the things our Safety Council reviewed during their site visits.

CHAPTER 24.

Business Continuity

Most businesses have some form of an Emergency Response Plan which lays out the steps to be taken that will minimize threats to life, property, equipment, and the environment during different types of emergencies.

In 2013, after some of our fleets had to deal with major flooding in Ft. McMurray, Calgary, and Toronto, PWT recognized that we were overdue on developing viable Business Continuity Plans at each of our Branches.

We recognized that when a disaster hits, it might not only effect our facilities, but could also affect many of our suppliers as well. We needed to ensure we could respond immediately, and keep our fleets operating.

And so at each Branch we:

- identified the critical services, equipment, or products that must be provided (drivers, buses, fuel, parking, communications, etc.)

- listed the different types of threats (natural disasters, strikes/protests, terrorism, cyber-attack, pandemic, fire, etc.)

- made plans and developed procedures that as much as possible ensured the critical areas above were available at all times

- made assignments, trained employees, conducted drills, and performed yearly audits

We needed to make sure our fleets could continue to: a) offer services to our clients; b) bill our clients for the work performed; and c) receive and deposit payments from our clients for that work.

Little did we know at the time that it wouldn't be long before our Business Continuity skills would be put to the test. In May of 2016, what started as a bit of smoke south of Ft. McMurray, turned into a major raging wildfire that eventually consumed much of the area, and became known by firefighters as the "Beast".

At the time, our Diversified Transportation (DTL) operations in the area included 7 facilities, 357 motorcoaches, 144 yellow buses, 77 light vehicles, and over 1,000 computers and communication devices.

The DTL team did an amazing job of staying one step ahead of the fire as it ebbed and flowed around the Ft. McMurray area. We were able to provide bus service in the areas that were not on fire, as well as provide evacuations for the parts of the community being threatened.

When the fire finally petered out, our facilities had smoke and ash damage, but we had not lost a single bus. An amazing testament to the people and the planning of DTL.

Later on we debriefed our Ft. McMurray team to see what could be learned from their experiences:

Tips on Business Continuity Plans From the DTL Ft. McMurray Fire Experience

- Don't put this off, it can happen to you

- Identify and preplan safe zones where you will be able to relocate your fleet. Get approvals & agreements in place in advance

- Have multiple sets of keys for every one of your facilities. Keep spare sets both off site locally and off site out of the city (DTL wasted a huge amount of time trying to track down keys)

- Make sure that someone is regularly checking to ensure that all facility door locks are working (DTL found that several doors would not lock so had to use parked vehicles to block)

- Get someone that is out of the critical operational response to look after admin support such as tracking down people, tracking down where all vehicles are parked, capturing/ billing work being done, etc.

- Develop specific shut down procedures for each facility, such as which electrical, water, gas, heat/cool, lights, etc., gets turned off and which gets left on, etc.

- Look for possible things that could be done to protect the facilities, such as turning on the lawn sprinkler system during a fire, etc.

- Ensure you have up to date employee contact and emergency contact information on file. Have an agreement in place with employees about how and who will be contacted in an emergency (This was one of DTL's biggest stresses because often the data wasn't current)

- Make sure your key staff are able to, and know how to access the computer system remotely

- Have spare charged cell phone batteries available for key staff, and possibly also have a couple of spare cell phones ready

- Challenge the inventory that you have in company vehicles (DTL only vehicle loss was an IT service vehicle, but it contained 30 computers that were destroyed)

- Hold debrief meetings and capture learnings to be implemented

We also found that our insurance company was a great resource. They had lots of Business Continuity materials available, and offered to put on workshops.

CHAPTER 25.

Insurance Risk Control Visits

We felt that it is important for us to develop a strong relationship with our insurance company and our insurance broker. It is in our best interest to ensure they are knowledgeable about what we are doing, as well as how and where we are doing it.

Part of building that relationship is recognizing that the Risk Control Dept. of the insurance company will want to visit some of our facilities to confirm what is being insured, and to observe the programs we have in place to mitigate the risks.

So we welcomed the occasional Insurance Risk Assessment Site Visit. It is another set of eyes that can provide feedback and observations about risks and about programs. By being transparent about how we do things and how we manage/control the risks, our broker is better able to negotiate competitive rates at renewal time.

Here is an example of some of the areas the insurance risk control staff will look at on the fleet side:

-    Number and type of vehicles

- Are any dangerous goods handled?

- Are personal vehicles used for company business?

- Is there any personal use of company vehicles?

- Are vehicles leased on rented?

- The zone and radius of operations

- Is any freight being transported?

- Driver information

- Driver training program

- How drivers are monitored and supervised

- Loss records and analysis

- Vehicle maintenance and inspection program

- Management controls

But often their biggest concern is the buildings. Here is an example of the areas they will want information about on the property side:

- Description of the types of work done at the facility

- Construction type of the building(s)

- Who occupies the building(s)?

- Are there proper fire separations between different parts of the building?

- What are the hazards, and how are they controlled?

- What type of security protection is in place for employees?

- What type of security protection is in place for visitors?

- How is theft and burglary protected against?

- How are the premises monitored, inspected, and maintained?

CHAPTER 26.

Training

Human Resources, Training, and Safety are different. They are three separate distinct disciplines. But they do overlap, and should be linked together.

Actually, in many smaller companies these three areas are often lumped into one position. One person is tasked with recruiting, screening, orientation, on-going training, safety performance, and maybe even discipline (these staff get really good at changing hats).

This is a book about safety, so I won't delve into the HR or Training areas in too much detail. But here is how they are linked into our safety programs at PWT.

Human Resources

Safety staff have always had a love/hate relationship with the driver hiring process. We want to ensure recruiters pick talented, stable, resourceful applicants who are good, safe drivers and who take the challenges of the road in stride.

But often our industry experiences driver shortages, and so sometimes recruiters just need to put "bums in seats".

For years we looked for a magic wand. A tool that would help us reliably pick the best driver applicants, and would do it simply and quickly. Then - Ta Dah! - we discovered a great personality assessment tool.

In partnership with the industry, the developers of this product had put together a predictive analytics tool which apparently measures a variety of personality traits that have been linked to the unsafe behaviors which can lead to incidents and injuries on the road and in the workplace.

Using this tool has helped us identify and avoid applicants with at-risk tendencies. Which to a safety guy is music to my ears because we used to hire a lot of our problems. Now the personality assessments are an integral part of our hiring process, and over 6,000 potential new hires have been evaluated.

Not only do we hire better drivers, but the assessment tool helps speed up the screening process. And impressively, our employee turnover rate has dropped by 20%.

Training Centre

In 2007, as a result of a new contract requirement, DTL Edmonton created the "Diversified Professional Driver Training Centre", with the mandate of recruiting, screening, hiring, and training the bus drivers needed for this contract.

A few years later, when the project came to an end, it was decided that the Training Centre would be given a new mandate to become a centre of training excellence for the whole Pacific Western Group of Companies. The name was changed to the "PWT Bus & Coach Training Centre".

Although for the most part each Branch had their own training staff, the Training Centre established company wide training resources, had their courses and instructors accredited by the MCPCC (Motor Carrier Passenger Council of Canada), created industry leading training manuals, and in the next chapter we'll talk a little about their most ambitious, and successful project, the MTU.

For several years the Training Centre was a very busy place. But as emerging technologies began to percolate into our industry, we recognized that it was time to move with the times and embrace new innovations in the training field.

In 2014 it was announced that the Training Centre was being transitioned to become the "Centre of Innovation and Excellence (CIE)". It would continue to offer driver training, and operate the MTU, but it would also aggressively expand into technology-based platforms, including on-line course offerings.

As their name suggests, the CIE, utilized new recruiting technologies, new screening technologies, and new tablet-based training technologies. Additionally, they used Learning Management Systems to create and deliver online content, including a WHMIS 2018 course, a WCB Management Tips Session, and Frontline Supervisors Course.

Driver Training

I realize I am a little biased, but in my view the Training Dept. primarily exists to provide a service to Safety.

Whether working with new hires, or performing post-incident follow up training, the bottom line is that training must create a measurable difference in driver performance.

The goal is not about how many sessions have been conducted, not about how many students have been processed, not about how complete the curriculum is, and not about whether the instructors and content have been certified (although all of those things are admirable).

For me, the bottom line is about developing competencies in drivers that will reduce the possibility of them being involved in a collision, an incident, or a violation.

For a time we had a few instances where drivers who had a collision were put through an extensive defensive driving course, and/or a serpentine close quarters maneuvering course, and/or MTU training. But within a year some of them had another collision (in some cases several).

One of things we found was that the Training Dept. was often out of the loop. They were sent a driver to fix, but had not been given any information about the safety investigation or what specific areas the driver needed help with.

So they just put every driver who arrived on their doorstep through a generic A to Z defensive driving course, hoping that somehow enough of the problem area would be covered and make a difference.

Seems to me that trainers would be far more successful at changing behavior if they were in the loop with safety, and knew the specific areas they should be targeting.

Here is another area where technology is helping us take great strides forward. A few years back we started to use a tablet based software training management package.

It had all the usual bells and whistles such as record keeping, scheduling, testing templates, etc. Also, being able to use it in real time during an actual on road training session is a cool feature.

However, what I like best about the product is that each part of how to drive a bus or motorcoach is broken down into individual step by step competencies. For example, making a right turn would be broken down into preparation before arriving at the intersection, starting the turn, monitoring progress through the turn, exiting the turn, and resuming the trip.

This makes a great resource for the trainer when providing instruction, and also is a great template for assessing driver skills in real time on the road.

Again, for me, when all is said and done, the Training Dept. exists to develop competencies in drivers that will minimize collisions, incidents, and violations.

CHAPTER 27.

Mobile Training Unit (MTU)

Way back in 1929, the "Link Trainer" became one of the earliest, and best known flight simulators for the Allied forces. It had a generic cockpit with working instruments; a pneumatic motion platform driven by inflatable bellows that provided pitch and roll; and a vacuum motor that provided yaw.

During WWII approximately 10,000 of these simulators were produced and located in the USA and Canada. They were used to train 500,000 new pilots for the war effort.

Over the ensuing years flight simulators have become increasing sophisticated and realistic. They are made for almost every brand of commercial airliner, and of course for all types of military aircraft. Commercial pilots can actually accumulate logbook hours for their time on a flight simulator.

As the cost of the technology came down, simulators began to be developed for a variety of other industries as well. Using simulators for training instead of actual vehicles is now often less costly, and it provides opportunities to train no matter what the weather conditions are like outside.

But one of the main hallmarks of a simulator is that you can perform all types of dangerous, risky, and maybe even stupid maneuvers and experience the consequences, without any harm to people or equipment.

It is this feature that has attracted law enforcement, first responders, public works, and a range of truck, bus, and motorcoach operators to add simulators to their training programs.

We were fortunate that our President recognized that a driving simulator would have a significant impact on reducing the number and severity of our collisions. Arrangements were made to purchase a bus specific driving simulator from one of the industry leading manufacturers.

Our new simulator could be configured to train either motorcoach, school bus, or transit bus operators. But with Branches spread across much of the country, we struggled with where it should be located.

One of the obvious options would have been to install it in the Training Centre. But we quickly dismissed that idea as the costs and complexities of the logistics of moving thousands of drivers located all over the country to and from Edmonton didn't make any sense.

Once again our President came to the rescue. Through his contacts with a well-known entertainer coach provider, he was able to purchase an entertainer motorcoach that had just come off service. It was a perfect host for our Driving Simulator, and now we would be able to extend simulator training to every PWT driver, at every Branch, in every location.

We arranged to have the crew's bunk beds and the star's master bedroom removed. And in their place installed the driving simulator and a 12 person classroom. On June 28, 2010, Pacific Western proudly unveiled the Mobile Training Unit (MTU), a first of its kind in Canada.

Since that launch, the MTU has visited every facility and Branch across Canada, some of them several times. Thousands of motorcoach, school bus, and transit operators have been able to practice driving in poor weather, in tight parking spots, in city traffic, going down steep hills, being surprised by a moose, etc.

One of early success stories came from a motorcoach operator who was able to practice on the MTU how to regain control if a front tire blew at highway speeds. This is a rare occurrence that most operators are unlikely to experience in their entire careers.

But you guessed it - a few weeks after completing his MTU training, he was driving with a full load of passengers on the highway, when without warning the right front steer tire blew. His training immediately kicked in, and he was able to bring the unit to a safe stop on the shoulder.

It's no surprise that as a Canadian company, the winter driving module has perhaps been the most useful training the MTU provides. It helps our drivers feel confident, comfortable, and prepared as they get ready drive in snowy and icy conditions each year.

Also, the MTU is a great ambassador for the PWT brand. It has participated in a variety of client, industry, and community events. The hands on experiences of driving a bus in all kinds of conditions never ceases to impress, especially potential bus driver applicants, and potential new clients.

CHAPTER 28.

Root Cause Investigations

In my view, one of the silliest things our industry does after an accident is to perform a collision review to determine "preventability". In reality most times they are just determining fault. If the driver did something wrong, the accident is deemed to be "at fault" or "preventable".

Although these terms are often interchanged, they actually don't mean the same thing at all. One is about blame, liability, and punishment, the other about causal factors. One is about the driver, the other about systems and process.

In many companies once it is decided that the driver was "at fault", he/she is disciplined, and most times is also put through a generic defensive driving course. Apparently either or both of these measures are supposed to fix whatever was wrong with the driver.

After the suspension has been served and re-training accomplished, the driver then resumes his/her duties, the accident file is closed, and everyone goes back to what they were doing before.

But how does that take us anywhere? It often is just a revolving door process because the root of the problem is never discovered or addressed.

Of course drivers make mistakes. We know that because accidents happen. Maybe it would make a lot more sense to figure out why the mistake was made in the first place. That way we can perhaps do something about minimizing the possibility of it happening again.

When an accident happens, often a variety of experts attend the scene. But whether it is the Police, DOT, Insurance Adjusters, Reconstruction Specialists, etc., they really are only interested in finding out who is at fault, who is to blame, who gets the ticket, and who is going to pay.

Internal collision reviews, on the other hand, need to go deeper and look beyond the driver. We need to know the "Whys". The process of asking why can take the investigation step by step from the direct cause(s), to the indirect cause(s), and finally to the root cause(s), which is nearly always about the system.

Here is a simplistic example I found from a white paper dealing with the "5 Whys":

"A fatal crash occurred". WHY? "The vehicle skidded and lost control". WHY? "The road surface was wet and very slippery". WHY? "The wet skid resistance of the road surface was too low". WHY? "The aggregate used in building the road did not meet specifications". WHY? "The testing and quality assurance regime put in place by the material provider was not followed".

As each "Why" is asked, you can see how quickly we move away from the driver, and go deeper and deeper into the roots of the crash.

The fix in this case would be to ensure better monitoring and testing was performed, and quality assurance measures and standards were written into the material provider's contract - a more effective and far reaching result than simply blaming the driver for losing control on a slippery road.

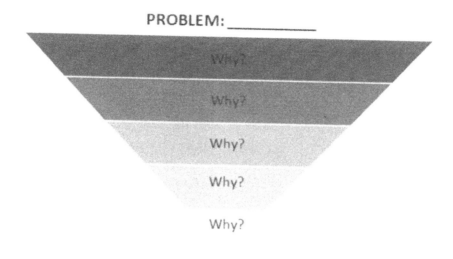

PROBLEM: _____

ROOT CAUSE

CHAPTER 29.

Workers Compensation Claims Management

One of the responsibilities universally hated by most of our managers has been looking after Workers Compensation Claims.

In a way you can't blame them. It is frustrating when a family doctor tells an injured worker to take two weeks off without even conducting an examination or without diagnosing the type or extent of the possible injury. And family doctors often put roadblocks in place to make it more difficult to get a worker back on the job through modified work assignments.

It seems that some WCB claims staff, as well as some family doctors think that the company is the enemy, and that it doesn't care about its people. They apparently have already made up their mind that the company is somehow at fault, and that they are not going to cooperate with us to get the worker back to work quickly. It almost seems that they are looking for a way to punish the company for what has happened.

But despite those frustrations, we try to help our managers deal more effectively with the process. However tempting it might be, just putting our head in the sand and washing our hands of the whole thing doesn't really help move things forward. And it can get expensive.

Yes, once in a while you will have an employee who might try to take advantage of the system. But by and large, most of our employees want to get well and get back to work. They are just as bewildered by the claim process as our managers are.

So we had one of our Safety Managers who was experienced in this area develop some tips to help supervisors manage a WCB claim from the initial report submission, right through to getting the worker fully back to work.

WCB FILE MANAGEMENT TIPS

What to do when the injury is reported:

- Manage the claim – don't expect the claim to manage itself – employer owns the injury

- Gather information – talk with your employee

- Does your employee want to see a doctor?

- When the employee does not want to see a doctor they must return to work

- Do not allow the employee to go home

Type of Injury:

- Traumatic Injury is caused by a specific incident
  - o Slip and fall
  - o Collision injury

- Progressive Injury a condition of pain that will worsen over time
  o Repetitive strain
  o Lower back pain from driving

- Another type if injury is an unreported injury. If you don't know about it – you can't manage it

OIS Clinics – Occupational Injury Services
(OIS clinics are available throughout Alberta)

Advantages:

- Clinic is familiar with the company modified work program

- Doctor will speak directly with the supervisor after the assessment to discuss restrictions

- Doctor will follow up with the employer after each visit

Open communication allows for effective management of the claim

Provide the doctor with the correct information:

- Provide a letter to the doctor explaining that modified work that is available

- Provide a form asking the doctor to fill out the restrictions for the employee

- Develop an open communication relationship with the doctor

Modified Work:

- Should always be readily available – keep the employee coming to work – don't let them sit at home

- Meaningful work – but designed to encourage the employee to get back to their normal full duties

- Employee to sign a Modified Work Contract immediately (can be found on the WCB website)

- Employee works the same number of hours and receives the same pay

- Employer to provide training for the modified work position when necessary

- Employees are still held to the same expectations while on modified work (arriving to work on time, performance)

Anyone on modified work is still accountable for work performance.

WCB Adjudicators and Case Managers:

- Develop a relationship with your WCB team

- Best practice – invite them to your location

- Provide a physical demands analysis for the position

- Talk with the adjudicator if you're having problems with the employee.

- The more knowledge they have about our company, the better they will also manage the claim

Positive Communication:

- Each time you talk with your employee talk the facts and don't allow emotions to get involved

- Caring about your employee will return him/her to duties sooner

- Make a point to follow up with your employee:

  o Talk with them after each doctor visit – ask how they are feeling

  o Discuss increasing the physical demands to the modified duties as the injury is getting better

  o Remind them they are important, and we need them back to full duties

- When talking with WCB it should always be positive and supportive of your people

Managing the Cost Claims:

- Modified work will reduce your costs on each claim and this will lower your experience rating:

  o Paying the wages up front means that you will not pay for it later through higher premium costs

- When an injury is not progressing ask your adjudicator – is there further testing?

- Managing the claim means following up

Best Practices:

- Always have modified work available

- Positive communication – employee, doctors, WCB team

- Develop relationships – employee, doctors, WCB team

- Attend seminars through WCB

- Have someone assigned to manage the claim and communicate with the operations team

- Always have your incidents recorded

CHAPTER 30.

Small Group Safety Meetings (SGSM)

The traditional safety meeting usually involves a supervisor (or more often a safety specialist) standing up at the front of a classroom, telling a somewhat disinterested audience of employees how things should be done.

To be fair, occasional formal safety meetings, with an agenda of information that needs to be passed along to employees, is of course required, or even mandated.

But if you really want to find out what is going on, and develop some ideas on how to improve things, you need to have some informal conversations with your frontline staff.

As the expression goes, it's not rocket science. The folks who are actually doing the work are in the best position to make some meaningful observations about hiccups, and can contribute golden nugget ideas on how to improve things.

After realizing we really didn't have an organized process in place to regularly listen to our people, we developed a template for what we eventually called "Small Group Safety Meetings":

- An informal ad hoc meeting

- With three to twelve frontline staff

- That runs about 15 min to 30 min

- Where safety is the focus

- Which is led by a frontline supervisor

- Where observations about the hiccups and the golden nugget ideas are captured

For example, a shop lead hand might wander into the break room at the end of the morning coffee break, and find five or six shop staff finishing off some donuts. He/she might say, "Folks, last month's KPI just came out, and I was surprised to see that our Branch had twice as many slips and falls than normal. If you have a couple of minutes, I'd like to hear your observations. What is going on? Have you slipped? Where do you see the problems? What has changed"?

After a handful of minutes bouncing around if and why there is a problem, then switch to asking about what kinds of things they think might help reduce those slips and falls.

This sounds deceptively simple. But it is usually not that easy for supervisors because they tend to be better at telling, not so much with asking or listening.

The key to whole exercise is giving employees a chance to be heard, and a chance to contribute.

Obviously, the company will not use every suggestion. But it should come as no surprise that Branches who regularly hold Small Group Safety Meetings, tend to have the best KPI results, and they also have staff who are more engaged and satisfied with their work.

Instead of workers nodding off in their chairs while some safety guy or gal dryly rambles on about rules and regulations, the SGSM has them up on their feet and contributing.

Did you know that according to a Gallup survey of 100 million workers, only 30% feel engaged and are enthusiastically involved in their work? That means 70% of the work force doesn't really feel much connection with their work. Often it is because they don't receive recognition or encouragement, and are seldom asked for their opinion.

What do you think the numbers are like at your place of work?

People need to feel important. They will attempt to go up, jump off, go over, or slide down a variety of obstacles faster than anyone else - just to be noticed.

Here is a quote from one of my presentations at the 2010 PWT President's Safety Summit: "Our success in attracting the right people, having them stay with us, and having them perform well, hinges on our managers knowing them, engaging them, listening to them, and responding to them".

Find ways to listen to your people. They have great ideas.

CHAPTER 31.

Annual PWT Safety Conference

When I joined PWT back in 2008 they had been holding a Safety & Loss Control Meeting each year. The President, the Board of Directors, and about a dozen of the key safety staff throughout the organization were invited to a retreat where they huddled for two days of shop talk.

The agendas included a report card overview, discussions about the challenges ahead, and a wish list of things they hoped could/should/ would be accomplished.

Although these meetings were held with the best of intentions, the problem was that the safety staff had mistakenly thought that they were in charge of safety. They thought they would be the ones that moved safety forward. They thought it was up to them to plan, carry out, follow up, and enforce safety initiatives.

This became very clear during a case study exercise I put on the first time I attended one of these meetings. The case study described a fictitious shop that had some young workers in the wash bay who weren't using PPE when handling a very corrosive cleaner. The case study laid out that both the Shop Foreman, the Maintenance

Manager, and the Branch Manager had observed these workers using this chemical without gloves or goggles, but had not done anything about it.

The question I posed was, "As the Safety Officer for the Company, what are you going to do about it"?

You might have guessed it - the response from most of our group was that they would march in with guns blazing and shut the wash bay down. They would organize and conduct a debrief meeting where they would, in no uncertain terms, tell all the players what was what. Then they would put on a training session for the wash bay workers, add a more strongly worded policy to the policy manual, and threaten the managers that if it happened again they could face enforcement action - Yikes!

None of our group mentioned that perhaps a more effective approach would have been for the Safety Officer to quietly take the Shop Foreman aside to relay the observation about the wash bay workers, to explain the significant potential for harm to them, to lay out a few possible options, and then to offer to assist as needed.

To put it bluntly, these Safety & Loss Control Meetings really weren't going anywhere because the people attending them didn't have the ability to actually make things happen. As you saw in one of our prior chapters, it is the frontline workers and supervisors that develop and produce safe performance.

So in 2010 we transitioned away from the old style Safety & Loss Control Meeting, and held the first annual PWT Safety Conference. This time, in addition to the President and the Board, we had each Line of Business VP, along with their Branch Managers, the Operations Supervisors, and a Director of Maintenance for each Line attending.

The only safety staff at the Conference were the VP of Safety and a Director of Safety from each Line.

The attendees were the people who actually planned, supervised, carried out, and followed up on the work of the PWT organization. During the Safety Conference it was the operations staff who were reviewing challenges, workshopping potential fixes, and laying out action plans to accomplish their safety performance objectives.

The safety staff were just there as a resource, to coordinate the process, and to offer support and technical assistance.

The 2010 PWT Safety Conference marked a fundamental shift in how safety was done at PWT. It was a watershed moment in PWT's "Journey to World Class Safety".

If there is one thing I hope you the reader takes away from this book, it is this principle that safety is owned by the people who are doing the work, not the safety staff.

CHAPTER 32.

PWT Safety Council

Most of us don't like being told what to do. It doesn't matter if the advice is for our own good. And it doesn't matter if the person doing the telling has incredible credentials and experience. If someone is telling us to do something, we often put up a fight.

At PWT there are three levels of organization: Branches, Lines, and Corporate, all wanting to have some say on how things are done.

In the early days we struggled to find a way for the safety staff at all three levels to work together on safety issues. Despite the best of intentions, there always seemed to be tension between the various players. When Corporate Safety took the lead, there was some resentment by the Lines. And when Line Safety took the lead, Corporate worried that the Lines didn't get the whole picture. And Branch Safety just felt ignored either way.

Once we realized that it wasn't safety staff who should be driving safety solutions, the PWT Safety Council came together quickly. It is attended by the President, the four operational Line VPs, the three Directors of Safety, and the VP of Safety. Originally chaired by the President, it is now chaired by one of the Line VPs.

The Safety Council agenda includes reports on a wide range of company safety programs such as KPI, CoS, NSC, COR, Carrier Profiles, etc. From these reports it becomes apparent which areas are working well, and which areas may need some strengthening.

After a group discussion, the Line VPs make decisions on what is to be done by whom and when. They make and prioritize the resource assignments, and drive the execution, governance, and follow up. The Safety Directors provide coordination between levels, as well as support and technical expertise. And the President liaises between the Board and the Council to ensure this work is meeting Board expectations.

The immediate benefit of the Safety Council was better cooperation between the three levels, and more effective and timely responses to safety challenges. But also the Safety Council was created strategically, recognizing that at some point in the not too distant future that I'd be retiring. And that going forward the Safety Council would for the most part take the place of a VP of Safety.

That's exactly what happened. As planned, the PWT Safety Council has now assumed most of the roles and responsibilities that used to be looked after by myself.

Here are Council key accountabilities from the "Council Terms of Reference" document:

- Compliance – Provide oversight of compliance with safety regulations and legislation in the jurisdictions where PWT operates. Identify, monitor, and mitigate Line of Business exposure. Ensure process is efficient and effective.

- Reporting - Monitor monthly safety Key Performance Indicators. Track and conduct trending analysis. Highlight early warnings and potential risks.

- Safety Management System – Oversight of the design, controls, and effective upkeep.

- Systems Improvement – Encourage better information (accessible, reliable, timely). Improve, automate, integrate processes. Track progress, get early warnings, know results. Enable faster response. Support compliance.

- Influence Policy, Behaviors, Standards, Systems – Promote better results. Seek outside experience and knowledge.

- Monitor Culture of Safety in the Organization – Uncover and address issues and concerns.

- Mentor, Coach, and Support the Organization.

- Ensure continuous improvement and application of best practices

- Achieve Unity and Order by maintaining the purity of the message and a consistent method of delivery. Provide the translation between the Objectives of the Board when it comes to the delivery of safety programs and monitoring execution

- The Board sets the safety Objectives; The Executive sets the Targets, and the Safety Council develops Strategy and coordinates Implementation.

CHAPTER 33.

The Annual PWT Safety Perception Survey

This book contains chapter after chapter describing the variety of safety initiatives and programs PWT put in place during "Our Journey to World Class Safety". As you can see, there were/are many moving parts, that working together have advanced safety performance forward.

However, we found that it can be really easy to get so wrapped up in the managing of all those programs, that we can lose touch with the reason we are doing all of this stuff in the first place, which is to help frontline employees make good choices that will help them avoid having any collisions or incidents.

We may think we are pretty good at designing, developing, and implementing safety programs. With a little bit of pride, we think our programs look good, sound good, and work good. But we also recognize that the true test of how effective programs really are, is whether they are making it all the way out to the frontlines.

So, every April, we perform a PWT Safety Perception Survey. It is a completely anonymous online survey, hosted by a recognized survey management provider. We provide the weblink code, and then employees can access the survey on their smartphone, tablet, or PC. We also set up computers in the lunchrooms of our facilities for those who don't have any other access.

For each of the thirteen statements in the Survey, the respondent answers that they either, Strongly Agree, Moderately Agree, Moderately Disagree, Strongly Disagree, or if they feel none of those apply they can answer N/A. Additionally there is space below each statement to provide comments and feedback.

Every manager, supervisor, and employee is encouraged to participate. And amazingly we consistently get over 80% response rate across the entire group of companies.

We tabulate and analyze the results, and by using the same thirteen statements each year, we can track, year by year, where we are falling short, and where progress is being made.

Some of the best feedback we receive about our programs is from the comment section. It is really helpful to hear unfiltered feedback about how we are doing.

We found that sometimes our managers got a little defensive about employee observations. They would argue that they had done training, posted materials, and had involved staff in the rollout, so the employee must have been wrong in observing that they hadn't been told.

But here is a "newsflash" - people's perceptions are not facts. Perceptions are how people feel about things, they are just opinions.

We already knew that our managers, for the most part, were rolling out safety initiatives and programs fairly well. The survey is not so much about measuring what was being done. The survey is more about how our employees feel about their work.

No matter how well we think we have communicated something, it only works if the message is being received. We learned that responding to feedback about an area that needed strengthening was not about doing more, it was about engaging more. We found that the highest scores and the most positive feedback came at Branches where our managers had established strong connections with their people.

Here is the survey we use each year:

PWT Annual Safety Perception Survey Questions:

1. My supervisor understands the safety challenges I face in my work

2. If I see something unsafe, no matter where, I report it

3. Safety always takes priority over moving passengers on time

4. My supervisor talks to me about safety at least every month

5. I have been told about the hazards in my job and how to avoid them

6. I know our KPI goals and how we are doing each month

7. When I tell my supervisor about a safety concern, it gets fixed right away

8. Safety policies, standards, and rules have been clearly explained to me

9. I know about the Fleet Safety and Workplace Safety yearly audits and why they are done

10. In the last six months I have been involved and discussed safety issues with my supervisor

11. I intervene when I see a co-worker performing an unsafe act

12. I have read and understand the PWT Safety Vision Statement

13. I have received value from attending a Safety, Toolbox, or Small Group Safety Meeting

SECTION 3.

Our Results

CHAPTER 34.

Our Results

As I mentioned at the beginning of this book, when I joined the Pacific Western Group of Companies as their VP of Safety, I was given a two part mandate:

a) help improve safety performance across all parts of the PWT organization

b) help PWT become the industry leader in bus and motorcoach safety

Over the years, little by little, our programs matured and were better executed. We tightened things up in the way we delivered programs, and we more accurately identified the areas still needing attention. Our implementation and follow up was focused and therefore effective.

a) help improve safety performance across all parts of the PWT organization:

In 2017 we broke all Company records:

Preventable Collisions – a record low

Driver Violations – a record low
WCB Incidents – a record low
WCB Lost Days – a record low
TIF Rate – a record low
Preventable Collision rate – a record low
Small Group Safety Meetings – a record high

For motor carriers, the most common measure of fleet safety performance is the Preventable Collisions per Million Mile Rate. Because this measure is a rate, it can be used to make comparisons between all different types and sizes of organizations. And in our case, this was a very useful tool to assess how our Lines and Branches were stacking up against each other.

In 2008, the Preventable Collisions per Million Miles Rate was a fairly mediocre number, and PWT weren't even capturing data about many of their parking lot dings.

By 2019 all preventable collisions were being properly captured, and the rate had gone down drastically – **a 64% decrease!**

Another example of how much progress had been made was WCB Lost Days. This is a measure of how many days employees were not able to work because of a workplace injury.

In 2010 we experienced an all-time high in the number of lost days - a dismal number in the hundreds. By 2017 we had made a dramatic improvement - **a 96% decrease!**

"Yikes! - this stuff really works".

And by the way, it definitely is not a coincidence that in the year we had a record low number of incidents, that was also a year that we had a record high number of Small Group Safety Meetings.

The more times we listen to our frontline employees, the more we learn about what's really going on, and the more real world solutions we discover.

b) help PWT become the industry leader in bus and motorcoach safety:

Developing and promoting a unique and well-known Brand is so important for a business.

A study quoted in a Globe and Mail article a few years ago indicated that "…research suggests that children as young as three are quick to identify a brand and decipher its message. In the study group 93% identified the McDonald's golden arches, 77% identified the Pepsi red, white, & blue button, 53% identified Shell's shell, and 80% identified the Toyota horned logo."

Try it yourself with this list of products: motorcycles, soup, tissue, rice, and oats. I'm guessing most of you thought of: Harley Davidson, Campbell's, Kleenex, Uncle Ben's, and Quaker.

Using the "Steak vs. Sizzle" approach, we communicated, shared, and promoted our safety programs to the industry, and we were rewarded.

Over the years we have been:

- invited to contribute regular articles for BUSRide magazine

- invited by a major vehicle manufacturer to audit their factories

- invited to audit a number of the more well-known US motorcoach operators

- elected to executive of Bus Industry Safety Council

- served on several industry association committees

- invited by NTSB to testify as a subject matter expert

- invited by SAE and a variety of industry associations to put on presentations

- invited to travel to Lloyds of London to speak to a number of umbrella/excess insurers

- confirmed to be top ranked bus company by our insurance company

- received International Motorcoach Group (IMG) Safety Award; BUSRide Magazine Safety Award; IMG "Operator of the Year" award; Videographer Award of Distinction;

American Bus Association Leadership Recognition Award; and the Norm Littler Memorial Safety Award

Mission accomplished - the Pacific Western Group of Companies has become synonymous with bus and motorcoach safety.

"Safety" has indeed become PWT's brand.

SECTION 4.

Next Steps

CHAPTER 35.

Next Steps

Every journey has an end. And this one did too.

I have tried to share a travelogue of the trip. We prepared, we departed, we had a few hiccups along the way, but eventually arrived at our destination. And PWT attained what it started out to accomplish.

And now it is time to move on, both for PWT and for me. It is time for both of us to transition.

For me, it is time to transition into semi-retirement. As I look back, I am grateful for the work I have been able to do with PWT. And thankfully, now as a consultant, I am still able to accomplish the occasional project for them.

For PWT it is time to grow the company. Programs, structure, management team, and resources have all come together now at the right time, and the company is poised and ready to take some significant steps forward.

And so the new PWT safety objective will be to "Sustain" what has been accomplished. As the company grows and expands, safety performance needs to keep pace, and the company needs to continue to be a leader in bus and motorcoach safety. "Sustaining" PWT's industry leading safety performance will still be a significant challenge.

Perhaps a few of you reading this will remember the Ed Sullivan Show. It was an early TV variety program that ran from 1948 to 1971. It aired every Sunday night and featured a wide variety of performers and acts.

One of the most popular acts was Erich Brenn, a plate spinner. His routine consisted of spinning eight plates on four foot-long sticks. Once he got them all spinning, the trick was to go back and forth, keeping them all spinning, and ensuring none fell off.

Sure enough, as he was on one end of the row, some of the plates on the other end began to slow down and started to wobble uncontrollably. This would get a rise out of the audience, who thought for sure that some of the plates would soon fall and smash into dozens of pieces. But just in the nick of time, Brenn would swoop down the line and get all the plates spinning again, resulting in a sigh of relief from the audience.

As you've seen from the many chapters in this book, there are a lot of moving parts to the PWT Safety Program. Now that PWT has all these "plates" spinning, they will have to become very good plate spinners to keep everything humming along.

One of the ways that has been accomplished has been through using a RACI chart. We identified all the various components of our programs, and identified our key staff. Then we matched up staff positions with the new roles we expected them to take on as the company transitioned to "Sustaining" safety performance. These would either be R (responsible), A (accountable), C (consulted), or I (informed).

PWT Safety RACI
External
Industry Relationships
Community Liaison
Government Relations
External Communications
Insurance Company Liaison
Client Liaison
Litigation Liaison
Incident Response
Compliance
Internal
Strategy Development
Leadership
Executive Resource
Policy and Procedure Development
Claims Management
Reporting (KPI)
Safety Management
Improve Efficiency (CoS)
Systems Improvement
Road Fleet Safety
Facilty Workplace Safety
Facility Environment (hazardous materials)
Collision Investigation
Workplace Incident Investigation
Environmental Investigation
Support Business Development
Research
Internal Communications
Provide Advice
Influence Policy, Behaviours, Standards, Systems
Liaison with Training
Monitoring 'Pulse' of Safety in the Organization
Mentoring/Coaching / Support

The transition to these assignments was accomplished in 3 phases. Phase 1: July – December 2017 was the preparation stage. Phase 2: January – June 2018 was the actual transition to the new RACI roles. And Phase 3: July – December 2018 was for fine tuning and last minute adjustments.

As these steps were accomplished, the baton of safety leadership was passed on from the VP of Safety, to the "Three Main Pillars" of the transition:

- Branch Managers – "Own"

- Directors of Safety – "Support"

- Safety Council – "Coordinate"

At the end of 2018, the PWT "Journey to World Class Safety" formally transitioned to "Sustaining".

It has been a wonderful trip. Like any good story it contained interesting characters, things expected as well as big surprises, visits to places far and wide, both the mundane and the extraordinary, sometimes with peaceful progress but occasionally packed with drama.

But definitely worth the time and effort. A great success story. And one to be treasured.

SECTION 5.

Final Words

CHAPTER 36.

Final Words

Growing up, one of my favorite cartoon characters was Mighty Mouse, a miniature flying super-hero with a cape, much like Superman.

In each episode a variety of characters were always getting into a pickle. Sometimes they were threatened by a natural disaster, sometimes they were threatened by bad guys. But either way, in desperation, a call would go out to Mighty Mouse to come and rescue them.

Once Mighty Mouse arrived and hovered over the scene, he would survey the situation and then call out in a loud voice, "Here I come to save the day"! and then he swooped in to make a dramatic rescue.

To be honest, most safety staff fantasize about swooping in to "save the day". We wish we could show up with super-powers that could immediately fix whatever was wrong.

But regrettably that is not how it works in the real world. Getting out of a safety pickle most times is more of a process than a single event. And seldom is there one solution that dramatically turns things around overnight.

In fact, large one shot safety programs that are introduced with a big splash are sometimes like watching whales. They look pretty magnificent while on the surface, and occasionally put on a great show as they rise above the waves and breach, splashing everyone in the process. But then they disappear underneath the waves, and are not seen again, often for a long time.

Similarly, although a big splash one time safety program gets everyone's attention for a little while, its effects are usually short lived.

Let's use another analogy, this time on land. Irrigation systems supply needed water to crops as they grow from seeds to maturity. Sprinklers are turned on during scheduled times each week to flood the fields with an allotted volume of water.

However, the process is not very efficient. Water is scattered everywhere, not just where it is needed, at the roots. The ground goes from having too much water when the sprinklers are on, to not having enough when they are off.

A much better delivery system is Drip Irrigation, which continually applies a small volume of water directly to the plant root zone where it is needed most. This eliminates runoff and evaporation, and is over 90% efficient.

While we are at it, let's do one more analogy - you've all heard the expression about taking "baby steps".

How do we as humans progress from being carried everywhere to driving the family car? - Lift Head, Roll Over, Sit Up, Crawl, Stand Up, Take First Steps, Intentionally Move Objects, Run and Jump, Use Utensils - Drive the Family Car.

Hopefully by now you are getting the message loud and clear - safety programs and initiatives that use small daily incremental activities, performed step by step, over a long period of time, are far more effective than short sporadic sudden bursts.

Many people today are drawn to promises of big results that will happen overnight. We're going to lose fifteen pounds, grow a head of hair, eliminate wrinkles, and get healthy all within a couple of weeks. And of course we're also going to get rich overnight by winning the lottery.

I don't think so. Success comes from simple, small, one by one steps, day after day. That may seem rather ordinary and unimpressive, but over extended time the results can be spectacular.

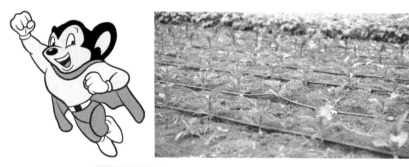

And let me finish with a few observations about "Becoming".

All of us are on a journey. Each day the experiences we go through add another chapter. Our lives ebb and flow as we enjoy success or struggle with challenges.

Often, after some time has passed, we look back with fond memories of both the ups and the downs of our career, and as we begin to make sense of it all, we can embrace the progress we have made through good and bad.

It is natural to occasionally daydream about bypassing some of the grief and already being at our destination. But it is the journey that provides the most meaningful experiences and satisfaction. We all need to be moving, and there is nothing quite like the feeling of progress.

Organizations are the same. The progress they make on their journey becomes their culture. And the organization is only viable when moving forward. A journey builds people, creates connections, gives purpose, allows expression, encourages contributions, and engages.

So by all means set challenging safety performance goals - big numbers that will signal success. But remember that the biggest benefit will come from the trip, not from the arriving.

The most valuable part of safety is the "Becoming".

ABOUT THE PACIFIC WESTERN GROUP OF COMPANIES

The Pacific Western Group of Companies, also known as Pacific Western Transportation, or just PWT, is a 100% family-owned group of bus companies that operates a fleet of almost 5,000 Motorcoach, School, and Transit Buses throughout much of Canada, and charters into the USA.

In addition to regularly scheduled services and charter work, PWT also has provided transportation services for large events including the Vancouver 2010 Olympics, 2015 Canada Winter Games, 2015 Pan Am and Para Pan Games, 2017 Invictus Games, and 2018 Arctic Winter Games.

In 1957, the founder of PWT, Robert Colborne, took over a fleet of 37 school buses that were operating in Red Deer, Alberta. He named the company, Prairie Bus Lines. And the rest, as they say, is history.

Other bus opportunities soon came his way, and over the ensuing years Bob either bought or created a variety of motorcoach, school, and transit bus companies. Instead of operating them all under the same name, or managing them all from a central corporate office, Bob's strategy was to use unique brand names that connected with the local communities, and then empower the local managers to run the operations.

As Bob continued to cobble together this decentralized group of bus companies, it eventually became the Pacific Western Group of Companies, with dozens of different brands, operating out of approximately 70 facilities across Canada. It grew into one of the largest bus companies in Canada, and is the largest privately-owned passenger transportation company in North America.

Originally the Branches were grouped and supervised by geographical areas. But eventually they were all were organized into four Lines of Business, each led by a VP:

The Motorcoach Line operates Alberta's premier intercity service (Red Arrow and Ebus) with a fleet of executive class Prevost motorcoaches. The PW Toronto division is an internationally recognized charter operator who has looked after the Pan Am Games, G8 & G20 Summits, and are the "go to" transportation provider for NFL, CFL, MLB, NBA, and FIFA sports events.

Additionally the motorcoach group operates a unique public-private partnership service (Northern Health Connections) to transport patients in smaller communities throughout British Columbia to the larger centers for medical specialist appointments and diagnostic testing.

The Employee Transportation Line moves thousands of workers to, around, and from oil, gas, mining, and construction projects, mostly in the Ft. McMurray and Edmonton areas. They dispatch more trips each day than any of Canada's major airlines.

The Student Transportation Line safely delivers over 70,000 kids daily to and from schools in a wide range of rural and urban communities across Canada. Their best known brand is Southland

Transportation which has a large footprint across much of Alberta. They also operate a paratransit door-to-door service for passengers with disabilities.

The Transit Line manages and operates a number of municipal transit systems, transporting over nine million passengers a year. They provided transit service for the 2010 Winter Olympic Games at Whistler, and the 2015 Canada Winter Games in Prince George, British Columbia.

The four Line of Business VPs, and their corresponding Branch Managers run the day-to-day operations, while the Corporate Office primarily provides finance, insurance, the purchase of vehicles & property, industry relations, support, direction, and strategy.

Bob Colborne passed away some years ago, but his legacy continues on through his family, with one of his sons, Michael Colborne, now serving as the Chairman and CEO.

Pacific Western Transportation
1857 Center Ave SE
Calgary, AB T2E 6L3
Canada
(403) 248 – 4300
www.pwt.ca

ABOUT THE AUTHOR

Stephen Evans served as the Vice President of Safety for the Pacific Western Group of Companies from 2008 through 2018, and was the architect of PWT's "Journey to World Class Safety". Under his leadership PWT significantly reduced the number of collisions and incidents, and PWT became known as an industry leader in bus and motorcoach safety.

As a well-known transportation safety subject matter expert, thought leader, writer, mentor, and facilitator, Stephen has had considerable success in helping companies significantly reduce the number of vehicle collisions and worker injury incidents.

He has conducted safety audits of a number of the leading bus and motorcoach operators in Canada and the USA. Additionally he has conducted safety reviews at manufacturing plants, parts distribution facilities, and service centers.

Stephen has been a long term member of the Bus Industry Safety Council (BISC). He served as the Chair of its Vehicle Technical Operating Committee, followed by terms as Secretary, Vice-Chairman, Chairman, and Immediate Past Chairman.

Recognition of his work includes the International Motorcoach Group (IMG) Safety Award; BUSRide Magazine Safety Award; IMG "Operator of the Year" award; Videographer Award of Distinction for his "Safety Flare" video series; American Bus Association Leadership Recognition Award; and the Bus Industry Safety Council's Norm Littler Memorial Safety Award.

In 2016 he began contributing regular articles for a column in BUSRide Magazine. These dealt with bus and motorcoach issues in a more practical way. He has also contributed articles that have appeared in several national magazines.

He has made presentations at a number of organizations including the American Bus Association Marketplace Conference, SAE Industry - Government Meeting; the Alberta Student Transportation Advisory Council (ASTAC); the Luxury Coach & Transportation Show (LCT); as well as a variety of industry meetings. Additionally, he gave testimony as a driver safety subject matter expert at the NTSB Truck & Bus Safety Forum.

Besides BISC, his association affiliations have included the American Bus Association, the United Motorcoach Association, the International Motorcoach Group, the Canadian Trucking Alliance, the American Trucking Association, the Alberta Motor Transport Association, International Society of Air Safety Investigators, the Air Transport Association of Canada, the Canadian Owners and Pilots Association, the International Civil Aviation Organization, the American Society of Safety Engineers, the Canadian Society of Safety Engineering, the Alberta Association of Safety Partnerships, and the Society of Automotive Engineers.

Stephen obtained a Bachelor's degree in Geography from the University of Lethbridge. He also obtained Canadian Registered Safety Professional (CRSP) accreditation; completed the Alberta Motor Transport Fleet Safety Management program; and participated in the Bus & Motorcoach Academy Safety Management Seminars.

He completed an Aviation Safety Management Diploma program from the Institute of Safety & Systems Management at the University of Southern California; took training at the Federal Aviation Administration's Civil

Aviation Medical Institute; completed National Transportation Safety Board investigation courses; and attended the Transport Canada Aviation Safety/Risk Management Program.

Besides a strong background in truck, bus, and motorcoach safety, he also worked in aviation looking after flight safety, cabin safety, ground safety, and emergency response for a Canada/US regional commercial airline.

Stephen is now semi-retired, but still occasionally provides transportation safety consulting to motor carriers across Canada and the USA through his company, Evans Safety Solutions Ltd.

Stephen Evans
Evans Safety Solutions Ltd.
213 – 3rd Ave E
Barnwell, AB T0K 0B0
Canada
(403) 915 – 5681
stephen@safetyevans.com

CPSIA information can be obtained
at www.ICGtesting.com
Printed in the USA
BVHW071934130421
604819BV00008BA/604

9 780228 849469